You won't believe what my wings are covered in. Head to page 72 to find out!
How small am I? Turn to page 84 to learn more!

TOTALLY RANDOM

QUESTIONS

VOLUME **5**

101 Incredible and Intriguing Q&As

Contents

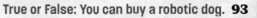

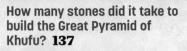

True or False:

#1

Astronomers discovered a planet made of **diamonds.**

lava life

Skies sparkle above a never-ending ocean of lava

ANSWER: **True**

FORTY LIGHT-YEARS AWAY FROM EARTH, ASTRONOMERS BELIEVE THERE IS A PLANET MADE OF DIAMONDS. Named **55 Cancri e,** the planet was discovered when scientists were studying the star that it orbits. **The planet's surface is made of mostly graphite, the same substance found in pencils.** But underneath the surface, they say, lies a thick layer of diamonds. What makes the planet perfect for creating these stones? For starters, its surface can reach temperatures as hot as 3900 °F (2149 °C). **The planet's solar system is also very rich in the carbon needed to make diamonds—** which suggests that the planet has lots of carbon, too. That, along with the high temperatures and pressure of the planet's atmosphere, makes it an ideal environment to produce diamonds. **Astronomers believe that this discovery has unveiled a whole new class of planets never seen before.**

Horses
can't vomit.

Crunchy!

#2

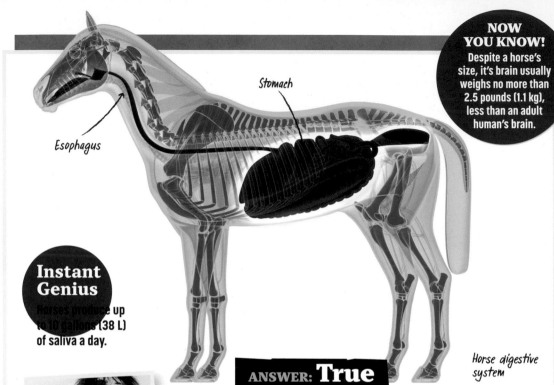

Esophagus

Stomach

Instant Genius
Horses produce up to 10 gallons (38 L) of saliva a day.

Horse digestive system

ANSWER: **True**

THE MUSCLES AROUND A HORSE'S ESOPHAGUS—THE TUBE THAT RUNS FROM THE THROAT TO THE STOMACH—ARE SO STRONG THAT ITS STOMACH WOULD EXPLODE BEFORE IT COULD VOMIT. This is actually very unusual because vomiting is a survival instinct in most mammals! **Though it may seem gross, throwing up allows mammals to get rid of toxins that have already entered the body.** Usually vomiting happens when the entrance from the esophagus into the stomach opens back up, allowing unwanted food material to travel back up the throat. **But a horse has such a strong esophagus, that vomiting is impossible.**

What is
California's
official state sport?

a. cross-country running

c. rodeo

b. surfing

Instant Genius

Big-wave surfers specialize in riding waves more than 80 feet (24 m).

NOW YOU KNOW!

Polynesians invented surfing. Olympic swimmer Duke Kahanamoku popularized it and helped turn it into a competitive sport in the early 1900s.

ANSWER: **b** **surfing**

USA 37

DUKE KAHANAMOKU

2002

SURFING IS THE OFFICIAL STATE SPORT OF CALIFORNIA, U.S.A. With more than 1,000 miles (1,609 km) of coastline, warm weather, and reliable waves, many California beaches have ideal surfing conditions. **Every year, several beaches in California host numerous surf events and competitions.** Spectators can even check out the Surfers' Hall of Fame in Huntington Beach. Surfing is a popular activity in a number of other states and countries around the world. **Some of the most unique places people have surfed include the coast of Antarctica and China's Qiantang River.** Surfing is enjoyed in both cold and warm weather, as long as waves are crashing.

Who was **Nintendo's famous video game** character Mario named after?

#4

a. the game's inventor

b. the son of the game's inventor

c. the man who rented Nintendo a warehouse

PLAYING CARDS

TRADE NAPOLEON 福 MARK

THE NINTENDO PLAYING CARD CO.

SHOMEN—DORI ŌHASHI,
KYOTO, JAPAN.

ANSWER: C **the man who rented Nintendo a warehouse**

NINTENDO'S FAMOUS VIDEO GAME CHARACTER MARIO WAS NAMED AFTER MARIO SEGALE, THE LANDLORD OF THE COMPANY'S WAREHOUSE IN THE 1980s. Segale made an impression on the Nintendo team during that time. **One day, the Nintendo team was debating the name for their plumber character when Segale stormed in and demanded they pay their overdue rent.** From that moment, the team decided to **name their character "Super Mario."** Segale's name wasn't the only thing to influence the character—his Italian heritage did too. When the character Mario speaks in the game, you can hear that he has an Italian accent. **Mario went on to become one of the world's most famous video game characters.** Segale was a very humble man, however. He did not talk much to his family or friends about his namesake character.

Instant Genius
The Nintendo company was founded in Japan in 1889.

#5

There's no place like home.

True or False:

Ligers can be found in the wild.

NOW YOU KNOW!
The average liger is 4.5 feet (1.4 m) tall and weighs around 1,000 pounds (454 kg).

ANSWER: False

Instant Genius

The cub of a male tiger and a female lion is called a tigon.

THE LIGER DOESN'T EXIST NATURALLY, BUT THERE ARE SEVERAL LIGERS IN CAPTIVITY. Ligers are the cubs of a male lion and a female tiger. **Lions and tigers almost never interact with each other in the wild, because lions mostly live in Africa and tigers live in Asia.** Although some lions and tigers do naturally live together in some parts of India, there has been no evidence of liger cubs being born. **Ligers are instead the result of lions and tigers having cubs together in captivity.** Because ligers can't have their own cubs, they're not considered a separate species.

Which of these natural features is there more of?

#6

b. stars in the Milky Way

a. trees on Earth

c. blue whales in the sea

Instant Genius

Because of light pollution, it's harder to see stars in cities than in the country.

ANSWER: a **trees on Earth**

EVEN THOUGH ONE-THIRD OF ALL FORESTS HAVE BEEN LOST TO DEFORESTATION, THERE ARE STILL MORE TREES ON EARTH THAN STARS IN THE MILKY WAY GALAXY—AND THE NUMBERS AREN'T EVEN CLOSE! There are an estimated 100 billion to 400 billion stars in our galaxy, and more than 3 trillion trees on Earth. To estimate the number of trees on our planet, scientists used a combination of satellite images, digital models, and ground measurements. The process scientists use to estimate the number of stars in our galaxy is less certain. First, they had to calculate the mass of our galaxy and how much of that mass stars take up. Then they had to guess the average mass of all the stars in our galaxy. This number dramatically changes the final estimate, which explains the large range.

NOW YOU KNOW!
Fewer than 25,000 blue whales live in the ocean. They swim in all the oceans of the world except around the Arctic.

#7

Shark and human eyes

are nearly identical.

ANSWER: **True**

IT TURNS OUT THAT MOST SHARK EYES HAVE DEVELOPED IN A VERY SIMILAR WAY TO OUR OWN. In a human eye, the cornea is the dome-shaped area on the outer, center part of the eye. It allows light to enter, and is responsible for keeping vision clear and protecting the inner eye from damage. **Shark corneas are similar enough to humans' that doctors are testing their use to help patients who have diseases or damage in their eyes and need transplants.** Without this option, a patient has to wait for a human eye donor. **But shark corneas, which are made of superstrong fibers, may turn out to be a better option.**

Which diseases did

George Washington

survive?

#8

a. smallpox and malaria

b. diphtheria and tuberculosis

c. all of the above

An 1800s painting of draining blood, also known as bloodletting.

ANSWER: **c all of the above**

GEORGE WASHINGTON SURVIVED MANY DISEASES. The list includes smallpox, malaria (six times), diphtheria, tuberculosis (twice), dysentery, and pneumonia. This is an impressive accomplishment for Washington because, at the time, doctors didn't know how to effectively treat many of these ailments. One remedy to treat smallpox back then included consuming the ashes of burned toads! Another doctor recommended drinking lime or lemon juice to treat a fever. **The lack of proper treatment, and the seriousness of these diseases, would make Washington's survival seem unlikely. In the late 18th century, 3 out of every 10 people who had smallpox died.** And even today, tuberculosis is the world's deadliest infectious disease, killing more than 65 percent of the people who catch it.

Instant Genius
Thanks to vaccine programs around the world, smallpox was eradicated by 1980.

In the United States, what percentage of **dog owners** let their pets sleep in bed with them?

a. 10 percent   **b.** 50 percent   **c.** 74 percent

Am I snoring?

Instant Genius
Small dogs dream more than larger dogs.

ANSWER: **C**

74 percent

ONE STUDY SHOWED THAT ALMOST 75 PERCENT OF AMERICAN DOG OWNERS LET THEIR DOGS SLEEP WITH THEM IN BED OR ON A COUCH. Snoozing with a dog in bed can make someone feel comforted and safe because they know that the dog will alert them of anything potentially dangerous. And that's not all. Although the dogs are dozing, scientists say that they might be dreaming, too. **Just like people, dogs need sleep to be mentally alert and physically strong.** Researchers tested the brain activity of sleeping canines and discovered brain waves that indicate similar sleep patterns to humans. **During deep sleep, pups may whimper, woof, or twitch their paws—all signs that your snoozing dog is dreaming.**

For each minute of the day, how much **rain falls to Earth?**

a. **10 tons**

b. **1 million tons**

c. **1 billion tons**

Meghalaya state in India

ANSWER: C **1 billion tons**

ABOUT 1 BILLION TONS OF RAIN FALL TO EARTH EVERY MINUTE.
This rain does not cover Earth evenly, though. Some places get very little rain, such as the Atacama Desert in Chile, where only half an inch (1.27 cm) of rain falls a year. Others get lots of rain, like Meghalaya state in India, where the average annual rainfall is 467 inches (1,186 cm)! One reason for these differences is the uneven heating of Earth's surface. The sun warms the equator more than any other part of Earth because it's closest. The hot, humid air at the equator rises and creates clouds that eventually release rain. **This is why regions at and around the equator experience large amounts of annual rainfall and are often dense with vegetation and forests.**

Instant Genius

On one of Saturn's moons, called Titan, it rains methane gas.

True or False:

Your body can't sink in the
Dead Sea.

#11

Floating in the Dead Sea

NOW YOU KNOW!
The surface of the Dead Sea is the lowest point on Earth's surface. This sea is also the fifth saltiest body of water on our planet. The saltiest is the Don Juan Pond in Antarctica.

ANSWER: True

YOU CAN'T SINK IN THE DEAD SEA, WHICH GETS ITS NAME FROM THE FACT THAT NO ORGANISMS CAN LIVE IN IT. Why not? **It's too salty! The Dead Sea is about eight to nine times saltier than our oceans.** Salt adds mass to the water, which makes it denser than water in a bathtub or pool. **The denser the water, the easier it is to float in.** Though there's no sinking in the Dead Sea, the Dead Sea is shrinking. **That's because it is located in a desert that gets a lot of sunlight.** The sea shrinks about 3 feet (1 m) every year because water evaporates under the sun's bright rays and because water that feeds into the sea has been diverted for other uses.

"המקום הנמוך בעולם"
"أوطأ محلّ في العالم"
"Lowest Place On Earth"

חמי עין גדי
حمّام عين جدي
En Gedi Spa

True or False:

In some courts, a **bloodhound's** sense of smell can be used as evidence.

#12

The clue is under the flowerpot.

ANSWER: True

FOR HUNDREDS OF YEARS, BLOODHOUNDS HAVE BEEN WORKING HAND IN PAW WITH LAW ENFORCEMENT. If the police need to track a person's movements, they'll have a bloodhound sniff a piece of the person's clothing. The bloodhound can then create and remember an "image" of the scent in its brain. Some dogs have tracked odors for more than 130 miles (209 km) and that were 300 hours old! How do bloodhounds smell so well? They have about 230 million scent receptors in their noses—around 40 times more cells than humans have. The loose, wrinkly skin around their noses also helps them capture scents. In 2003, scientists tested the bloodhound's sense of smell and found it was so accurate that any trails they pick up could be useful in a court of law to prove a person's whereabouts.

Instant Genius
Dogs can smell at least 1,000 times better than humans.

What was the first toy to be advertised on TV?

a. Barbie

b. Mr. Potato Head

c. Lego bricks

ANSWER: b **Mr. Potato Head**

MR. POTATO HEAD, ONE OF THE MOST POPULAR AMERICAN TOYS TODAY, WAS INVENTED BY GEORGE LERNER IN 1949. Lerner came up with the idea of plastic face pieces that kids could poke into fruit or vegetables to make silly expressions. Toy makers feared that encouraging kids to play with their food would seem wasteful, however, especially after years of food rationing during World War II. Thank goodness a toy company saw potential. **On April 30, 1952, Mr. Potato Head became the first toy to be advertised on television.** It went into production just a few days later and became a huge success, selling over a million toys in the first year.

The HASBRO Guide to America's TOP TEN TOYS!

Mr. and Mrs. POTATO HEAD
the joyful toy of 1001 faces!

Where is the fastest muscle in the body?

a. jaw

b. eye

c. hand

ANSWER: b eye

EACH EYE HAS A MUSCLE CALLED THE ORBICULARIS OCULI, WHICH IS IN CHARGE OF SNAPPING YOUR EYELID CLOSED. If something were to come hurtling toward your eye—such as a stick from a tree branch— your involuntary reflexes would kick in, triggering the eyelid to close to protect you. **The orbicularis oculi can shut the eye in a tenth of a second.** Although you probably use this muscle only rarely to shield your eyes from danger, it's also the muscle you use to blink. **We blink as many as 15 to 20 times a minute, which adds up to 28,800 times per day.** The rate at which people blink varies due to factors like the environment, gender, age, and health. **But according to studies, women blink more often than men, and babies blink slower and less often than adults.**

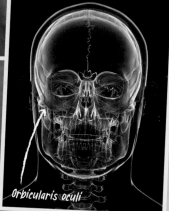

Orbicularis oculi

How many hairs per square inch does a

house cat have?

a. between 10,000 and 15,000

b. between 35,000 and 45,000

c. more than 60,000

Too many to count!

ANSWER: c **more than 60,000**

MOST HOUSE CATS HAVE ABOUT 60,000 HAIRS PER SQUARE INCH (6.5 SQ CM) ON THEIR BODIES AND HEADS, AND DOUBLE THAT ON THEIR BELLIES! In comparison, humans have just 800 to 1,290 hairs per square inch on their heads. **Having dense fur helps protect cats from harsh elements in various climates.** In hot weather, a cat's fur acts as a natural sunscreen, protecting its skin from the sun. In fact, **a relative of the house cat, called the sand cat, can withstand temperatures as high as 124 °F (51 °C) and as low as 31 °F (–0.5 °C)!** Their fur prevents heat from reaching their body on hot days and helps trap in heat to keep them warm on cold nights.

Instant Genius

After a house cat sheds, the hairs take three to five months to regrow.

NOW YOU KNOW!

A house cat's whiskers are so sensitive that they can detect a change in air pressure. As air moves, their whiskers vibrate.

Sand cat

#16

In ancient Rome, only men could be gladiators.

Third-century mosaic of fighting gladiators

Instant Genius
The first gladiator games were performed during funerals.

NOW YOU KNOW!
Female gladiators were first allowed to fight because people thought they would bring humor to the battles.

ANSWER: **False**

ALTHOUGH RARE, FEMALE GLADIATORS DID FIGHT IN ANCIENT ROME. Starting in the third century BC a gladiator was someone who fought against another person or an animal in a coliseum for others to watch as entertainment. However, female gladiators only fought other females. Although many gladiators were enslaved people or accused criminals who were forced to fight, some gladiators chose the lifestyle. **Women had very little freedom at that time.** They were expected to follow their husband's or father's orders. **Though becoming a gladiator was extremely dangerous, some women chose this lifestyle to gain independence, fame, and money.** Unlike male gladiators, female gladiators were seen as unsuitable for marriage once they had chosen their roles. **After some time, however, female gladiators began to grow a fan base as more and more Romans came out to watch them.**

Which land mammal has a
lopsided heart?

a. **elephant**

b. **giraffe**

c. **rhinoceros**

ANSWER: b   giraffe

A GIRAFFE'S HEART WEIGHS ABOUT 25 POUNDS (11 KG) AND IS 2 FEET (0.6 M) LONG. **It's also very strong. Because the giraffe has an extremely long neck, its head is 6.5 feet (2 m) away from its heart, which is quite far.** This means the heart has to super-pump the blood to circulate it throughout the body and up that long neck. The left ventricle, or heart chamber, pumps blood all the way to the head, so it has adapted to be very muscular and thick. **Giraffes with shorter necks have thinner muscle walls in their heart because not as much pressure pushes down on the heart.**

In which country can you find people living on floating islands?

a. Australia

b. Peru

c. Argentina

Uros Tribe

ANSWER: b Peru

ON LAKE TITICACA IN PERU, THERE ARE MORE THAN 70 HUMAN-MADE FLOATING ISLANDS. **They are built by the Uros tribe, a group of people native to Peru and Bolivia that date back to before the Inca people.** The islands are made of layers of totora reeds woven into blocks. The bottom layer, beneath the water, decomposes as time goes on, which gives off gases that help the islands float. **The islands are tied to large wooden poles driven into the bottom of the lake.** This keeps them from floating away. The Uros people have to constantly add reeds to the top of the islands because the bottom layer quickly breaks apart. **Each island lasts about 30 years before a completely new one needs to be built.**

Lake Titicaca floating islands

Instant Genius

The largest islands in Lake Titicaca can house up to 10 families.

44

Lead can turn into gold.

#19

79
196.967

Au

Gold

82
207.200

Pb

Lead

ANSWER: True

SCIENTISTS HAVE BEEN ABLE TO TRANSFORM LEAD TO GOLD, BUT ONLY A LITTLE BIT—AND IT WAS VERY DIFFICULT. Lead and gold are both elements. **Elements are made up of different numbers of neutrons and protons, which are housed in the nucleus of an atom.** Lead has 82 protons in its nucleus and gold has 79. **Transforming lead into gold would require removing three protons.** This is super hard because the forces that hold an atom together are very powerful. Physicists tried exposing lead to high electrical currents to break the bond holding the atom together. That didn't work. In the next experiment, they bombarded lead with protons. The result? Scientists transformed the lead into the elements mercury, platinum, and gold. **In the end, however, the gold was radioactive and decayed in only a few minutes.**

Instant Genius

Gold is used on astronauts' helmet visors to block solar radiation.

NOW YOU KNOW!

Only 94 elements on the periodic table occur naturally. The others were made in a chemistry lab.

Which group of animals lived on **Earth** first?

a. **insects**

b. **dinosaurs**

c. **fish**

An illustration of some of the first living creatures on Earth

ANSWER: a **insects**

INSECTS EXISTED BEFORE DINOSAURS. **Scientists believe the earliest species of insect scuttled around Earth about 400 million years ago.** Dinosaurs came much later, about 245 million years ago, and are now extinct, whereas insects are still very much alive today. **Many ancient insects looked very similar to the insects we see now. However, ancient insects were gigantic!** There was a dragonfly-like species the size of a hawk, beetles as big as house cats, and millipedes as tall as five-year-olds. Why are insects so much smaller now? One theory: When these massive bugs lived, there was a lot more oxygen in the air, causing them to grow and develop at a much higher rate and scale. **As time went on and Earth changed, oxygen levels lowered, causing insects to stop growing so quickly.**

Instant Genius

The *Therizinosaurus* had claws that were 3 feet (1 m) long each.

#21

I thought I had nine lives?

How many years did the oldest recorded

cat

live?

a. **18 years**

b. **38 years**

c. **58 years**

Siamese cat

ANSWER: b **38 years**

Instant Genius

Cats don't meow at other cats, only at people.

THE AVERAGE HOUSE CAT'S LIFE SPAN IS ABOUT 15 YEARS, BUT AT LEAST ONE CAT HAS BEATEN ALL THE RECORDS. Creme Puff, pet to Jake Perry of Austin, Texas, U.S.A., lived an impressive 38 years and 3 days, making her the oldest cat ever recorded. Others, Bombay cats, for example, live about 20 years. So do Siamese cats. Perry was also the owner of the previous record-breaking oldest cat, Granpa Rex Allen, who lived to be 34. What's Perry's secret? Diet and exercise. He cooks eggs, turkey bacon, and broccoli to mix in with regular dried cat food. **Perry also constructed a series of tracks along the walls of his house for his cats to climb on for exercise and play.** He even converted his garage into a cat movie theater where he showed documentaries to stimulate their brains!

A **worm** can never dry out.

Can I get a glass of water?

ANSWER: **False**

WORMS DO NOT HAVE A SET OF LUNGS LIKE MOST ANIMALS DO—INSTEAD, THEY BREATHE THROUGH THEIR SKIN. To take in oxygen, their skin must be moist. **Moist skin also allows worms to stretch out and move through dirt or across surfaces. When it rains, worms come out of the soil to soak up the extra moisture, which helps them move more quickly.** However, when it stops raining, worms can get stuck on sidewalks and streets because they no longer have the extra water to help them scoot. When the sun comes out, worms can have trouble moving and breathing because their skin dries out, preventing them from taking in oxygen. **Luckily, most worms are quick enough to wriggle to safety before they dry out.**

Instant Genius

Worms can eat their weight in soil every day.

If you laid out your **lungs flat,** about how big would they be?

a. the size of a Ping-Pong table

c. the size of a tennis court

b. the size of a school bus

X-ray of human lungs

ANSWER: C

the size of a tennis court

THOUGH YOUR LUNGS ONLY WEIGH ABOUT 3 POUNDS (1.4 KG) AND FIT SNUGLY INSIDE YOUR CHEST, THEY ARE MADE UP OF LOTS OF MICROSCOPIC, SACLIKE STRUCTURES CALLED ALVEOLI. **The average set of lungs has roughly 300 million alveoli so when you lay them out flat, their combined surface area is about the size of a tennis court!** The alveoli are all connected by airways and, when lined end to end, the total length of the airways equals about 1,500 miles (2,414 km). **The alveoli's job is to take in the oxygen we breathe, deliver it to the bloodstream, and remove carbon dioxide from the bloodstream.** Around 1 to 2 gallons (3.8–7.5 L) of air typically move through the lungs each minute. Wow, breathtaking!

Alveoli

What do **bowerbirds** and **octopuses** have in common?

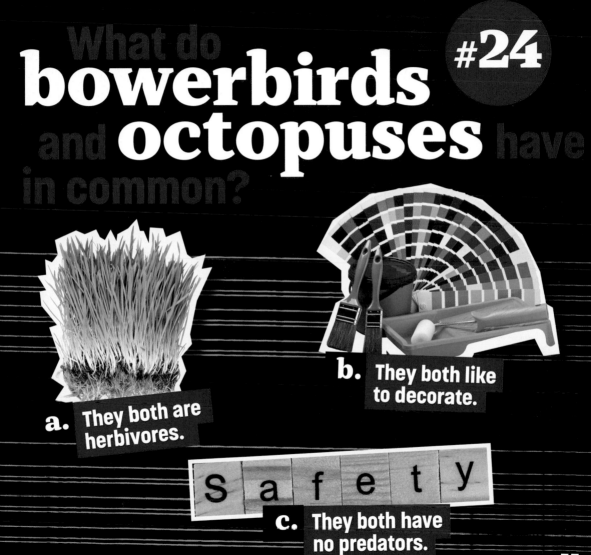

#24

a. They both are herbivores.

b. They both like to decorate.

c. They both have no predators.

Safety

ANSWER: **b**

They both like to decorate.

BOWERBIRDS AND OCTOPUSES BOTH CREATE ART IN THEIR NATURAL HABITATS. Male bowerbirds, found in Australia and Papua New Guinea, build large structures from sticks that look like large tepees, stretching 6 feet (1.8 m) across and 5 feet (1.5 m) high. Some birds will go the extra distance to add a carpet made of leaves, paint the sticks with berry juices, and decorate the entrance with rock patterns, snail shells, and colorful insects. **The only purpose of the structure is to attract mates, unlike the octopus that decorates its habitat for protection.** The octopus covers its den with shells and hard objects to camouflage with the seafloor and keep predators from attacking while they are nestled in their homes.

Why does **dry ice** burn your skin?

c. because it's radioactive

a. because it's hot

°C °F

50 120
40 100
30 80
20 60
10 40
0 20
10 0
20

0
10
20
30 20

RADIATION AREA

b. because it's cold

Dry ice

ANSWER: b **because it's cold**

DRY ICE, THE SMOKY STUFF THAT KEEPS FOOD FROZEN WHEN IT'S SHIPPED, IS MADE FROM FROZEN CARBON DIOXIDE, NOT WATER! **This is the same gas we exhale every time we breathe. Carbon dioxide freezes in its liquid form at –109 °F (–78 °C). The dry ice that forms is so cold that it causes something called an ice burn.** When dry ice encounters our skin, it freezes the water inside our cells and kills them, leaving burns similar to frostbite. That's why touching dry ice causes a painful stinging sensation. **Today, dry ice is often used in labs to keep chemicals cold.** You might also see it in a cauldron at a Halloween party, or as part of the spooky special effects in a TV show or movie!

Instant Genius
At room temperature, dry ice does not melt. It goes directly from a solid to gas.

26

What makes **cheetahs** different from other big cats?

a. They have spotted coats.

b. They can't roar.

c. They don't eat meat.

ANSWER: b **They can't roar.**

UNLIKE OTHER BIG CATS, CHEETAHS CAN'T ROAR. They are missing a special bone in their throat—called the hyoid bone—and the larynx, or voice box, both needed to make the loud sound. Instead of roaring, cheetahs purr like house cats and make high-pitched chirps. Cheetahs differ from big cats in other ways, too. **They have long tails for balancing when they run, large hind legs for leaping, eyes placed high on their heads, and claws that never fully retract—all features that other big cats do not share.**

NOW YOU KNOW!

The cheetah's body shape is more similar to a greyhound dog's than to that of other big cats.

27

True or False:

The
Hope
Diamond
is the biggest
diamond in the world.

Instant Genius
Diamonds are made of carbon.

ANSWER: **False**

The Hope Diamond

THE WORLD'S LARGEST DIAMOND IS THE CULLINAN DIAMOND, WHICH WEIGHED MORE THAN 3,000 CARATS WHEN IT WAS FIRST DISCOVERED. **Before it was cut, the Hope Diamond weighed just 112 carats.** However, the Hope Diamond—originally from a mine in India—still may be the most famous gem in the world because of its "curse." **According to legend, the curse started in 1666 when a Frenchman stole the deep blue diamond from a statue of the Hindu goddess Sita.** The diamond changed owners more than 10 times, and those who possessed it were supposedly struck with "bad luck." **The stone was named for British art collector Henry Philip Hope, who died in 1839, less than a decade after acquiring it.** Over a hundred years later, the diamond was donated to the Smithsonian Institution in Washington, D.C., U.S.A., where it resides today.

Henry Philip Hope

Who invented lacrosse? #28

a. ancient Egyptians

b. Native Americans

c. ancient Romans

ANSWER: **b** **Native Americans**

THE SPORT LACROSSE WAS INVENTED BY THE ALGONQUIN TRIBE, WHICH TODAY IS LOCATED ON THE BORDER BETWEEN CANADA AND THE NORTHEASTERN UNITED STATES. Gradually, other tribes along the eastern half of the United States started to play. **Each tribe had a different name for the sport, but the most common was baggataway, and the ball was originally a solid piece of wood.** Later it was made with animal fur covered in deerskin. **As many as 100,000 players would show up to play in competitive games that would last for days.** Much later, in the 19th century, Europeans saw the game being played in Canada for the first time. They took an interest and named the sport "lacrosse." **From there, lacrosse quickly gained popularity with the European settlements in Canada.** Some settlers brought the sport back to Europe and even introduced it to Queen Victoria of England.

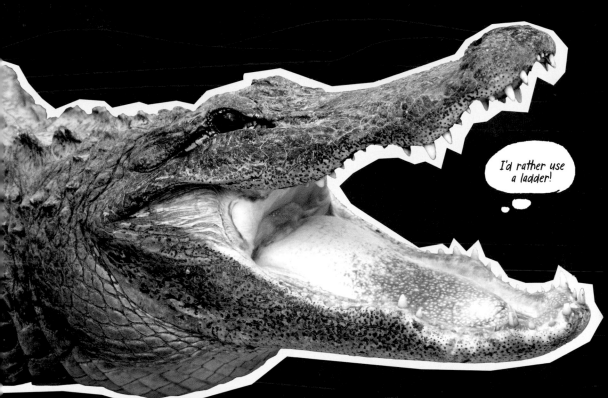

I'd rather use a ladder!

True or False:

Alligators

#29

can't climb fences.

NOW YOU KNOW!
Some alligators dig tunnels up to 65 feet (20 m) long for protection from the cold. They live in them during the winter, when they rest.

ANSWER: **False**

ALLIGATORS WALK ACROSS STREETS, CLIMB FENCES, AND SHOW UP IN PEOPLE'S BACKYARDS IN FLORIDA AND OTHER SOUTHEASTERN STATES. Why? As cities expand, the natural swamplands and marshes where alligators live are getting smaller, forcing these large reptiles into cities looking for food. **Alligators are very capable of climbing fences because they have large claws that can grab onto the fence and pull them up it.** They'll sometimes scale a fence in search of a tasty snack. Hungry alligators typically eat fish, turtles, or even snails. **As the top predators of the marshland food chain, alligators keep the fish and rodent populations in balance.**

BEWARE OF ALLIGATOR

What **statue** can you see if you visit a harbor in Copenhagen, Denmark?

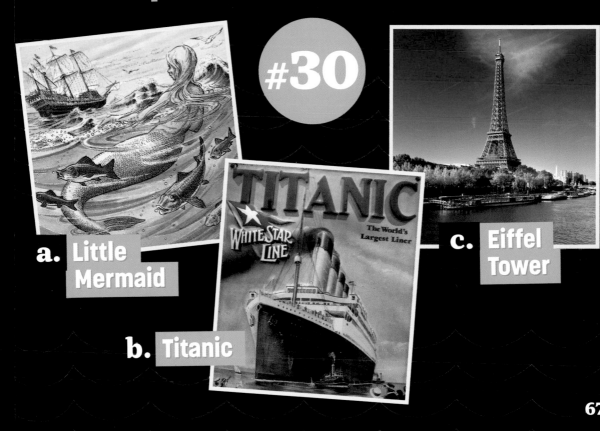

#30

a. Little Mermaid

b. Titanic

c. Eiffel Tower

67

Little Mermaid

STANDING AT JUST 4 FEET (1.2 M) TALL, THE *LITTLE MERMAID* STATUE SITS ON A ROCK IN THE HARBOR IN COPENHAGEN. The statue is the most popular tourist site in Denmark and one of the most photographed statues in the world. A Danish sculptor named Edvard Eriksen created it in 1909. **He based the statue on Hans Christian Andersen's fairy tale,** which did not have a happy ending. In fact, the mermaid never ended up with the prince and was turned into sea foam. This is the reason for the sad expression on the statue's face.

Instant Genius

The *Statue of Unity* in India is the tallest statue in the world, standing at 597 feet (182 m).

The Little Mermaid, Copenagen Harbour

Which is longer, the small or large intestine?

a. large intestine

b. small intestine

c. They are the same.

large intestine

small intestine

The total surface area of human intestines is about 430 square feet (40 sq m), or about the size of half a badminton court.

ANSWER: b small intestine

IN AN ADULT, THE SMALL INTESTINE IS ABOUT 16 TO 20 FEET (5–6 M) LONG, WHICH IS ROUGHLY 11 TO 15 FEET (3–4.5 M) LONGER THAN THE LARGE INTESTINE. It is called the small intestine because it's narrower than the large intestine, with a diameter of just 1 inch (2.5 cm). **But both intestines play a very important role in digestion.** They break down nutrients from food to be absorbed into the bloodstream. **Around 90 percent of food absorption happens in the small intestine. The large intestine absorbs any remaining nutrients, water, and electrolytes.** The leftover food that isn't absorbed in the large intestine becomes waste and leaves the body when you go to the bathroom.

#32

How many wings does a **butterfly** have?

a. two

b. four

c. six

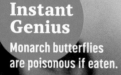

Instant Genius

Monarch butterflies are poisonous if eaten.

ANSWER: **b** four

BUTTERFLIES HAVE SIX JOINTED LEGS, TWO ANTENNAE, AND FOUR WINGS ATTACHED TO THE CENTER PORTION OF THEIR BODY, WHICH IS CALLED THE THORAX. The wings of a butterfly are covered in small scales that serve many purposes. Together, the scales create a larger wing mass, allowing heat to be captured and maintained to keep the butterfly warm. The scales also create the colors and patterns on the wings and body. Butterflies stand out to deter predators, who associate the bright colors with toxins and leave the butterflies alone to find less poisonous food elsewhere. The colors also help them blend into their colorful surroundings.

True or False:

Astronauts

#33

learn German to work at the International Space Station.

СОЮЗ

ANSWER: False

Astronauts preparing to head to the International Space Station

ASTRONAUTS HAVE TO BE FLUENT IN RUSSIAN, NOT GERMAN, TO WORK AT THE INTERNATIONAL SPACE STATION (ISS). Why? Astronauts travel into Russian territory to leave Earth and get to the ISS. This means that ground operators, who are the people guiding their journey, will all be speaking Russian. So astronauts would need to speak Russian in case they ever had an emergency on the ISS or on the way to and from it. **People who want to become astronauts don't have to speak Russian when they first apply.** If they are selected, they will undergo Russian language training. **To become fluent, candidates get one-on-one lessons with an instructor, take classes at a space station in Russia, and live in Russia for a short period of time with a Russian family.**

#34

One type of **coral** can make its own sunscreen.

NOW YOU KNOW!
Coral reefs cover just 1 percent of the ocean floor but contain more than 25 percent of all marine fish species.

Tide pools, Big Island, Hawaii

ANSWER: True

MOST CORALS PROVIDE A HOME TO ALGAE, WHICH ARE TINY LIVING ORGANISMS THAT THRIVE ALL OVER THE WORLD. In return, algae act as a natural sunscreen for coral, and they are also the coral's primary food source. **Hawaii's blue rice corals, however, produce a special protein that allows them to make their own sunscreen, so they can protect themselves from the sun's rays without any algae.** Why would corals need sunscreen? When climate change causes water temperatures to get too warm, corals get stressed and algae leave, so the corals are left without protection. **The corals will eventually turn pale, and most will die. This is called coral bleaching, and it's a major threat to coral reefs all around the world.** But for blue rice coral, the sunscreen it makes can prevent it from getting too stressed and dying.

Instant Genius
Corals also eat tiny floating animals called zooplankton.

What nationality was
Cleopatra?

a. Greek

c. Roman

b. Egyptian

ANSWER: a   **Greek**

A depiction of Cleopatra meeting Mark Antony, as imagined by an artist

THOUGH CLEOPATRA WAS THE QUEEN OF EGYPT, SHE WAS NOT EGYPTIAN. **Her family originally came from an area of Greece called Macedonia.** Cleopatra's father was one in a long line of Macedonian kings who ruled over ancient Egypt from 305 to 30 BC. **When her father died in 51 BC, 18-year-old Cleopatra inherited the throne alongside her 10-year-old brother.** As her brother grew up, he fought for complete control of the throne, forcing Cleopatra to leave Egypt. Determined to regain control, Cleopatra gathered troops and successfully took back leadership. **During her time away from Egypt, Cleopatra met Mark Antony, a Roman general. Antony eventually joined her in Egypt, and they ruled together.** When they attempted to take land from the Roman Empire, the Romans challenged and defeated the Egyptian forces, making Cleopatra the final Macedonian ruler of Egypt.

What are horse **hooves** made of?

a. bone

c. cartilage

b. keratin

ANSWER: b   keratin

KERATIN IS A HARD, PROTEIN-RICH MATERIAL THAT'S ALSO FOUND IN HAIR, WOOL, AND EVEN YOUR FINGERNAILS. **Keratin is the outer layer that covers almost all of a horse's hoof to protect the sensitive area underneath, called the frog.** Today, horses are given metal horseshoes that further protect their feet from sharp objects. **But just like your nails, a horse's hooves never stop growing.** That's why horses on ranches and farms usually get their hooves trimmed every six to eight weeks in the summer months. **This relieves strain on the horse's bones and joints, which is vital to their ability to walk.**

True or False:

A pineapple can eat you.

#37

ANSWER: True

NO, A PINEAPPLE WILL NOT GROW A MOUTH AND TAKE A BITE OUT OF YOU. But when you eat a pineapple, it digests a little bit of your mouth! That's because pineapples contain a digestive enzyme called bromelain. An enzyme is a type of protein that can speed up chemical reactions and break apart molecules in your body. Just like our bodies' digestive enzymes, bromelain can break down and digest cells that it comes into contact with. That's why you might feel a tingling sensation in your mouth after you eat a lot of the juicy fruit. Don't worry though, pineapples are still safe to eat, because the cells in our mouths heal quickly and our saliva contains natural painkillers. Once we swallow the pineapple, the acid enzymes in our stomachs can break down the bromelain.

Instant Genius
Figs, kiwis, and papayas all contain digestive enzymes like pineapples.

How many layers of skin does a **chameleon** have?

#38

a. 1

b. 4

c. 40

ANSWER: **b** 4

CHAMELEONS CONTINUE TO GROW THROUGHOUT THEIR ENTIRE LIVES. Every few weeks, they slowly shed their old skin cells to make way for new ones. These reptiles, like others around the world, **use the four layers of their skin to change colors based on their environment and mood.** The top layer of the chameleon's skin is actually transparent. The layer underneath it contains red and yellow pigments called chromatophores. The third layer contains cells that reflect blue and white light, and the fourth layer contains cells of brown melanin. (We also have melanin in our skin.) **The temperature and light cause all of these cells to go through chemical reactions, expanding and contracting due to the surroundings.**

Instant Genius

The smallest chameleon, the *Brookesia nana*, is 0.5 inches (1.3 cm) long.

#39

No continent
spans all four hemispheres.

Standing 709 feet (216 m) above the ground, Bloukrans Bridge bungee jump in South Africa is one of the highest jumps of its kind in the world.

Bloukrans Bridge, Africa

Nile River, Africa

ANSWER: False

Instant Genius

The world's longest river, the Nile River, flows through 11 countries in Africa.

THE CONTINENT OF AFRICA SPANS ALL FOUR HEMISPHERES: EASTERN, WESTERN, NORTHERN, AND SOUTHERN. It's the only continent with land crossing both the equator—the line dividing Earth into Northern and Southern Hemispheres—and the prime meridian, the line that divides Earth into Eastern and Western Hemispheres. **Africa is about 11.7 million square miles (30.3 million sq km) and covers a fifth of Earth's land surface.**

 #40

Your **brain** is about the size of your two fists put together.

Magnetic resonance imaging of human brain

NOW YOU KNOW!
It is a myth that we use only 10 percent of our brains at a time.

ANSWER: True

YOUR BRAIN IS ABOUT THE SIZE OF YOUR TWO FISTS PUT TOGETHER KNUCKLE TO KNUCKLE. **It weighs about 3 pounds (1.4 kg) once it's fully developed.** Considering their compact size, human brains are incredibly complex. **Brains contain around 100 billion neurons.** That's about half the number of stars in the Milky Way galaxy! Each of those 100 billion neurons is connected to about 10,000 other neurons, which adds up to one quadrillion connections in our brains! Information can pass between these neurons at speeds of 268 miles an hour (431 kmh). **The size of the brain tends to shrink as adults get older, though a smaller fully developed brain is not necessarily less intelligent than a larger fully developed brain.**

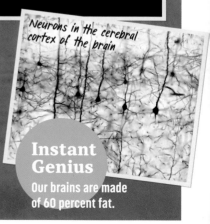
Neurons in the cerebral cortex of the brain

Instant Genius
Our brains are made of 60 percent fat.

88

#41

What happens to **smoke** in the weeks after a wildfire?

a. It becomes more toxic.

b. It becomes less toxic.

c. It remains the same.

ANSWER: a **It becomes more toxic.**

WILDFIRES ARE UNCONTROLLED FIRES THAT CAN BURN THROUGH FORESTS, FIELDS, AND COMMUNITIES. The smoke from wildfires often rises high into our atmosphere, allowing wind to carry it hundreds and sometimes thousands of miles away. Scientists have found that this smoke can become four times more toxic over time and linger for weeks after a fire. **Breathing in wildfire smoke can increase our risk of respiratory problems, heart attacks, and cancer.** Even people who live hundreds of miles away from a fire can still be at risk of facing these health concerns. Not all wildfires are bad, though. **A low-intensity, small-scale fire that is controlled by experts can help clear forests of dead vegetation and promote new growth.**

Instant Genius
Some plant species depend on wildfires to survive.

90

Why doesn't **aluminum foil** get hot?

a. It reflects heat.

b. It cannot hold heat.

c. It transmits heat.

Aluminum melts at about 1,220 °F (660 °C).

ANSWER: b It cannot hold heat.

IF YOUR PARENT OR CAREGIVER WRAPS FOOD IN ALUMINUM FOIL AND PUTS IT IN THE OVEN, YOU MAY NOTICE THAT YOUR FOOD WILL BE HOT WHEN IT COMES OUT, BUT THE ALUMINUM FOIL WILL NOT.

This is because aluminum cannot contain heat very well. Instead, heat passes through it quickly without warming it up. Because aluminum foil is so thin, it doesn't have the mass to hold a lot of heat. What little warmth it can trap is quickly lost to the surrounding air because it usually covers a large surface area.

#43

True or False:

You can buy a robotic dog.

ANSWER: True

IF YOU'VE GOT A COOL $75,000, YOU CAN PICK UP A ROBOT DOG NAMED "SPOT," MADE BY ENGINEERING FIRM BOSTON DYNAMICS. **The robotic pup has a 360-degree camera view, can complete programmed tasks, avoid obstacles, climb stairs, walk over rough terrain, and even dance!** Spot was designed to explore and work in places that are not safe for humans and to help businesses such as construction companies, power plants, and factories. **Scientists have discovered that four-legged robots are more stable than robots with one or two legs, so a mini-cheetah robot from Massachusetts Institute of Technology joins Spot in the robotic animal world.** Although this mini-cheetah is not for sale, it is currently the only four-legged robot that can do a backflip!

MIT's mini-cheetah

#44

Which physical ability began to fail artist

Claude Monet

over time?

a. hearing

b. eyesight

c. mobility

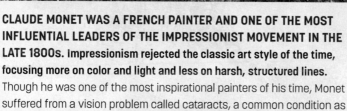

"Water lilies and Japanese bridge"

ANSWER: b **eyesight**

CLAUDE MONET WAS A FRENCH PAINTER AND ONE OF THE MOST INFLUENTIAL LEADERS OF THE IMPRESSIONIST MOVEMENT IN THE LATE 1800s. Impressionism rejected the classic art style of the time, focusing more on color and light and less on harsh, structured lines. Though he was one of the most inspirational painters of his time, Monet suffered from a vision problem called cataracts, a common condition as people grow older that gradually makes a person's vision foggy or less colorful. **Monet's cataracts impaired his ability to see colors like blue and green, giving his world a more red and yellow hue.** The effects of this can be seen in his paintings, as they shifted from blue-green tones to reds. **After 11 years, Monet underwent surgery to remove the cataract in his right eye, and his paintings returned to his usual cooler tones.**

NOW YOU KNOW!
Monet claimed that after his cataract removal surgery he could see UV light, which humans typically cannot see.

How well can dragonflies see?

a. better than humans

b. not as well as humans

c. It's a tie.

Nice detail!

ANSWER: a **better than humans**

DRAGONFLIES CAN SEE BETTER THAN HUMANS. How? They have up to 33 different light-sensitive proteins in their bodies that help with their vision, whereas humans have about nine. This means that dragonflies can see more details and colors than humans can. The insects can also see the world spherically because their eyes have roughly 30,000 sides, which help them see everything around them. Because of their keen sense of sight, dragonflies are considered the best predators on the planet. The insect captures more than 95 percent of the prey it targets. In addition to their super eyesight, dragonflies have another advantage: coloring that makes them difficult for prey to detect.

Instant Genius
Dragonflies can fly up to 60 miles an hour (97 kmh).

Which character is on a

NASA badge of honor?

a. Mario

b. Harry Potter

c. Snoopy

Apollo 1 crew

ANSWER: **C** **Snoopy**

THE SILVER SNOOPY IS AN AWARD ASTRONAUTS GIVE TO
NASA EMPLOYEES WHO HAVE CONTRIBUTED TO A MISSION'S
SUCCESS AND SAFETY. It's a very high honor, with less than
1 percent of NASA's workforce receiving the award every year.
But before it can be given, it travels in space! **An astronaut then
presents the sterling silver pin to an employee who helped them
on their mission.** The award was invented in the 1960s, after the
tragedy of the Apollo 1 mission that killed all three astronauts on
board. **It was one of the ways NASA tried to help astronauts build
stronger connections with the people helping them on the ground.**

Instant Genius

More than 15,000
people have
received the Silver
Snoopy Award.

True or False:

The temperature of a **sea turtle's nest** determines whether the hatchlings are male or female.

#47

What if I eat red algae?

ANSWER: **True**

WHETHER A BABY TURTLE IS BORN MALE OR FEMALE DEPENDS ON THE TEMPERATURE OF THE NEST. If the nest is below 81.9 °F (27.7 °C), the turtles will be born male. If the nest is above 87.8 °F (31 °C), the turtles will be born female. If the temperature fluctuates during the time the eggs are in the nest, the baby turtles will be a mix of both female and male. Because of climate change and warmer temperatures recently, more turtles are being born female. If the trend continues, one day the population could have so many females that there may not be enough males to reproduce with them.

Instant Genius
Leatherback turtles have existed since the time of the dinosaurs.

Which has the most bones?

#48

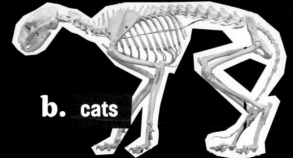

a. humans

b. cats

c. jellyfish

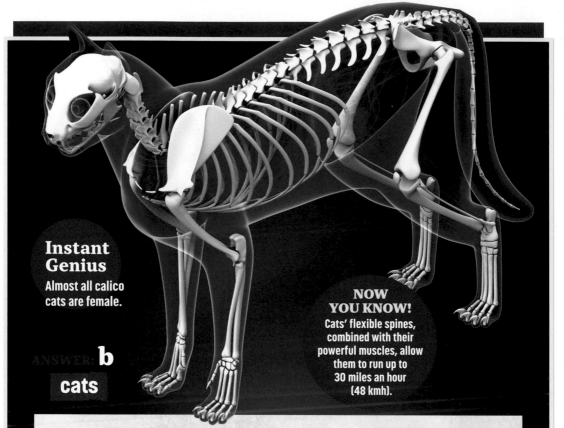

Instant Genius

Almost all calico cats are female.

ANSWER: **b**

cats

NOW YOU KNOW!

Cats' flexible spines, combined with their powerful muscles, allow them to run up to 30 miles an hour (48 kmh).

EVEN THOUGH THE AVERAGE HOUSE CAT IS MUCH SMALLER THAN A HUMAN, A CAT HAS MORE BONES. Cats have 230 to 250 bones, whereas adult humans have 206. Despite this difference, cats and humans have a similar skeletal structure. **But one obvious difference? Cats have tails. Humans have about 33 vertebrae in total, while cats have 18 to 23 vertebrae in their tails alone.** Cats also have one more pair of ribs than we do. Having so many bones in such a small body means that cats have many joints, which are formed where two or more bones meet. **These joints make felines extremely flexible and agile, which is why they are such excellent climbers and can land safely when they fall.**

#49

The dust under your bed has bits of insect poop in it.

ANSWER: True

NO, THOSE DUST BUNNIES AREN'T MADE OF FUR, OR EVEN FOOD. Most dust is made completely out of organic matter such as your own dead skin, cloth fibers, pet dander, and even insects, including their poop! Two-thirds of the dust in your house actually comes from outside. Inside, dust can collect on surfaces or it can float into the air we breathe. **Although dust may seem, well, disgusting, it doesn't pose any real threat to us.** That's because of the incredible filtering system built into our lungs. **When we breathe, the air first goes through tubes lined with cells that detect and filter out harmful dust.** Then whatever is left enters the lungs, where mucus traps most of the dust particles.

Instant Genius
The biggest way to cut down on dust in your house is to not bring shoes inside.

True or False:

#50

Watching TV can influence the color of your

dreams.

ANSWER: **True**

Instant Genius

Your heart rate and blood pressure both increase when you are dreaming.

NOT ALL PEOPLE DREAM IN COLOR. ABOUT 12 PERCENT OF PEOPLE SAY THEY DREAM IN BLACK-AND-WHITE, BUT THE PERCENTAGE DIFFERS ACROSS AGE GROUPS. Why? Several decades ago, television used to be only in black-and-white because the color technology hadn't been invented yet. Back in the 1940s, when color TV did not exist yet, people of all age groups reported almost never dreaming in color. Now, older generations who grew up watching black-and-white TV tend to dream more frequently in black and white, up to 25 percent of the time. **Younger generations who have only watched color TV, however, rarely report dreaming in black-and-white. Scientists know that our environment heavily influences our dreams, which could explain why TV viewing impacts how we dream.**

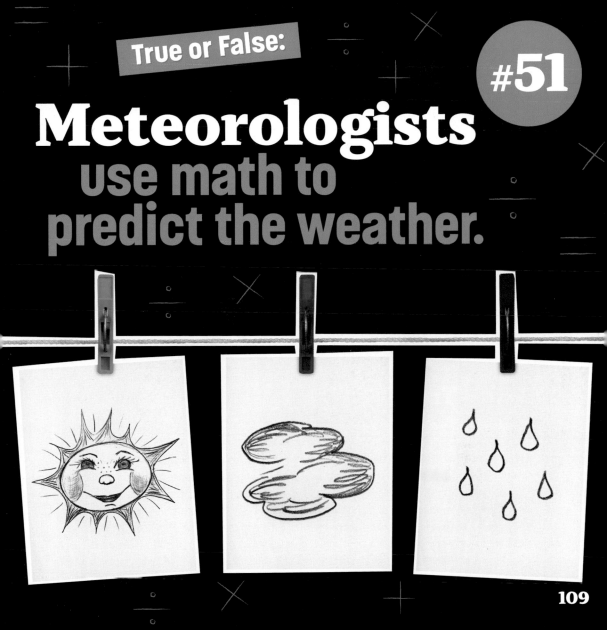

True or False:

Meteorologists use math to predict the weather.

#51

NOW YOU KNOW!
Meteorologists also use satellites to help them collect data about the weather. Some of these satellites face the sun to gather data about weather in space.

Instant Genius

In 1977, it snowed in southern Florida for the first time in recorded history.

ANSWER: **True**

WEATHER IS CONSTANTLY CHANGING AND OFTEN UNPREDICTABLE, YET IT AFFECTS THE LIVES OF EVERYONE ON EARTH. **This is why meteorologists use something called numerical weather prediction to forecast the weather as accurately as possible.** Numerical weather prediction is when meteorologists collect current observations of the weather—such as air pressure, wind speed, and temperature—and plug them into equations that can predict the weather up to 16 days in the future. **The meteorologists do not do these calculations themselves. They feed the weather observations into computers the size of school buses!** These computers can do 2.8 quadrillion calculations per second and they run all day, every day. **Besides weather, the computers can predict climate, hurricanes, ocean tides, flooding, and air quality.**

#52

True or False:

A killer whale

is a type of whale.

ANSWER: **False**

KILLER WHALES, ALSO KNOWN AS ORCAS, ARE TECHNICALLY DOLPHINS. In fact, they are the largest members of the dolphin family, sharing more physical characteristics with dolphins than with whales. Like dolphins, killer whales have heads that curve into a beak shape, which helps them glide through the water. Another distinction between killer whales and actual whales is that whales sing to communicate, whereas killer whales communicate by making clicking sounds—just like other dolphins. These powerful animals hunt for small creatures such as seabirds, but they also eat larger animals, including sharks and whales.

Which **continent** has the most countries?

a. **North America**

b. **South America**

c. **Africa**

ANSWER: C **Africa**

Katse Dam, Lesotho, Africa

AFRICA HAS 54 COUNTRIES—MORE THAN ANY OTHER CONTINENT IN THE WORLD. As the second largest continent in the world by surface area, Africa is larger than India, China, Mexico, and the United States combined. It is also the world's most diverse continent, home to thousands of tribes who collectively speak more than 2,000 languages, many of which are spoken nowhere else in the world. **Africa also has a wide range of climates and environments.** One of the most well-known regions is the Sahara, a desert that covers about a quarter of the continent. **Some other major habitats in Africa include tropical rainforests, savanna grasslands, highlands, and coral reefs.**

Instant Genius

Africa is the oldest inhabited continent on Earth.

What species of tree

is the tallest in the world?

c. giant sequoia

a. coast redwood

b. coast Douglas fir

Hyperion

Chandelier Tree, Chandelier Drive-Thru Tree Park

ANSWER: a   coast redwood

THE WORLD'S TALLEST SPECIES OF TREE IS THE COAST REDWOOD, WHICH CAN GROW MORE THAN 300 FEET (91 M) TALL.

The tallest individual tree, nicknamed Hyperion, is a staggering 379.7 feet tall (116 m). That's as tall as a 38-floor building! To keep from falling over, redwoods have an underground root system that stretches more than 110 feet (34 m) wide and intertwines with roots of other redwoods, which anchors them to the ground. How do these sky-high trees get so tall? **Some scientists think it's because they live in areas with steady, warm temperatures year-round and have access to plenty of rain and rich soil.** Not only are redwoods extremely tall—they can also live for hundreds of years, with some even living to be 2,000!

True or False:

#55

In Norway, schools and workplaces pause to watch the

Winter Olympics.

ANSWER: True

NORWEGIANS TAKE THE WINTER OLYMPICS SO SERIOUSLY THAT SCHOOLS AND WORKPLACES OFTEN TAKE A BREAK DURING THE DAY TO WATCH THE GAMES ON TV. **It's a good thing, because during the 2018 Olympic Winter Games, Norway broke an Olympic Winter Games record.** The country won 14 gold, 14 silver, and 11 bronze—39 medals total—surpassing the United States' record of 37 from the previous Winter Games. What makes this an extra impressive record for Norway? **Even though its population is 60 times smaller than that of the United States, Norway won 10 more medals than the United States that year.** Talk about raising the bar!

What percentage of your **body's bones** is in your hands, wrists, feet, and ankles?

a. 10 percent

b. 25 percent

c. more than 50 percent

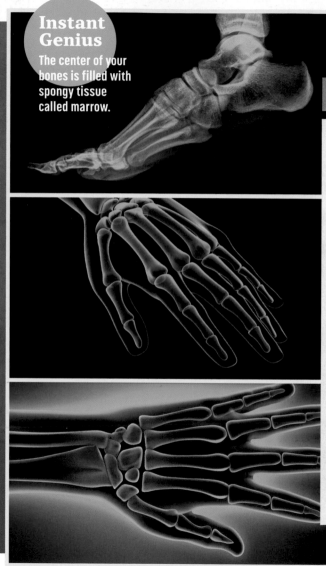

ANSWER: C

more than 50 percent

OF THE 206 BONES IN THE ADULT HUMAN BODY, 106 ARE IN OUR HANDS, WRISTS, FEET, AND ANKLES. Why are there so many bones in these places? **Many of the bones are very small. When two or more of these bones meet, a joint is formed.** The bones connect to the joint with a strong, stretchy tissue called a ligament. **Another tissue, called a tendon, connects the bone to muscle.** Each of your wrists has eight small, round bones. **Rather than a single joint, your wrist is made up of multiple joints, allowing you to rotate it in every direction.** Your bones, joints, ligaments, and tendons also work together in your hands, ankles, and feet. **This teamwork provides significant strength and flexibility in your ankles and feet, which are essential for standing, walking, and running.**

How does the spinifex hopping mouse survive life in the desert?

a. It doesn't need water.

b. It pees crystals.

c. It stores water underground.

Baby spinifex hopping mouse

ANSWER: b It pees crystals.

THE SPINIFEX HOPPING MOUSE LIVES IN THE HARSH AUSTRALIAN DESERT, AND IT HAS ONE OF THE MOST UNIQUE WAYS TO DEAL WITH DROUGHT AND DEHYDRATION. All mammals, including humans, have two organs called kidneys. The kidneys remove waste such as salt, extra minerals, acid, and any other excess fluids from our bloodstream in the form of urine, or pee. The mouse's kidneys are able to retain a much higher percentage of the fluids in its body than humans can. **Their kidneys do such as good job of filtering out minerals and keeping in liquids that their pee is often solid! This helps the mouse survive the frequent droughts that come with living in a desert.**

Instant Genius

Having big ears helps the spinifex hopping mouse's blood cool down, lowering its body temperature.

122

#58

True or False:

The **hottest planet** in our solar system is the one closest to the sun.

Mercury

ANSWER: **False**

MERCURY IS THE CLOSEST PLANET TO THE SUN, WITH A SWELTERING SURFACE TEMPERATURE OF 800 °F (427 °C). But Venus, the second planet from the sun, has an even higher average surface temperature of about 880 °F (471 °C). Why is Mercury cooler than Venus? Mercury has no atmosphere to retain the sun's heat. At night, the temperature on Mercury can drop as low as −290 °F (−179 °C). **However, Venus has a very thick atmosphere, filled with carbon dioxide and sulfuric acid that trap in heat, creating a greenhouse effect like the one we have on Earth, but one even more powerful.** This atmosphere gives Venus's surface incredibly high temperatures. Several countries have tried to land space probes on Venus, but few of the probes could withstand its intense atmosphere. **The longest-lasting one survived just two hours after landing.**

Instant Genius

Venus

On Venus, which rotates the opposite direction of Earth, the sun rises in the west and sets in the east.

How many legs do lobsters, crabs, and shrimp have?

a. 6 legs

b. 8 legs

c. 10 legs

ANSWER: C   10

LOBSTERS, CRABS, AND SHRIMP ARE ALL CRUSTACEANS, WHICH MEANS THEY ALL SHARE SPECIFIC FEATURES. **For one, they all have five pairs of legs.** The pair closest to the head is the largest and has big claws. **The claws help crustaceans catch and eat their prey, such as clams and small fish.** The two other pairs near the head have claws, too, but they are much smaller. **The final two sets of legs help the crustacean walk and swim.** But not all crustaceans can swim. Crabs, for example, walk on the ocean floor or hop from rock to rock. Lobsters and shrimp can swim because they have tails used to propel themselves forward.

NOW YOU KNOW!
The world's largest crab is the Japanese spider crab. Its legs can be as long as 14 feet (4.3 m)!

The original World Cup trophy had which

Greek goddess

depicted on it?

a. Aphrodite

b. Nike

c. Athena

127

Modern World Cup Trophy

THE WORLD CUP TROPHY IS AWARDED TO WINNERS OF THE INTERNATIONAL FEDERATION OF ASSOCIATION FOOTBALL (FIFA) WORLD CUP SOCCER TOURNAMENT. The first version was named the Jules Rimet Trophy, after the president of FIFA. The **trophy was made of gold and depicted Nike, the ancient Greek goddess of victory and a symbol of success for the Greeks.** The trophy was first awarded in 1930 to Uruguay after their World Cup victory. In 1970, Brazil won the trophy for the third time, granting them permanent ownership of the trophy and assigning FIFA with the task of creating a new Trophy. **This cup, now called the FIFA World Cup Trophy, is a 15-inch (38-cm) gold statue of two people holding up Earth.** Every four years, a brass copy is made and given to the winners of the tournament.

NOW YOU KNOW!
Brazil won the FIFA World Cup Trophy five times between 1930 and 2018, more than any other country.

Instant Genius
The Jules Rimet Trophy was stolen in 1983 and is still missing.

Iceland

is shrinking every year.

#61

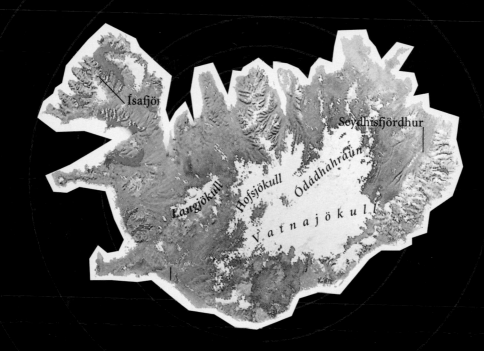

ANSWER: False

ICELAND IS GROWING ABOUT 2 INCHES (5 CM) EVERY YEAR. How? To begin, look at how the country formed. **Iceland was created by volcanoes in the ocean!** The island sits on top of where the Eurasian and North American tectonic plates meet. **About 60 million years ago, the two plates were moving away from each other at a very slow rate. As they split, they caused a fissure eruption, in which magma came out from underneath Earth's crust, floated to the top of the ocean, and cooled.** As the cooled magma built up over millions of years, the land that is currently Iceland was formed. Today, the two plates are still drifting away from each other. As the split becomes wider, more magma comes out of Earth's crust. **Once the magma cools and becomes rock, new land is formed.**

Instant Genius

At roughly 18 to 25 million years old, Iceland is one of the world's youngest landmasses.

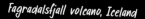

Fagradalsfjall volcano, Iceland

Bardarbunga volcano, Iceland

NOW YOU KNOW!

About two-thirds of all fissure eruptions in the world happen in Iceland. They can also be found in famous active volcanoes such as Mount Etna, Mauna Loa, and Kilauea.

The female **emperor penguin** takes care of her newly laid eggs.

62

Emperor penguins, Antarctica

ANSWER: **False**

THE MALE EMPEROR PENGUIN IS GIVEN THE VERY IMPORTANT JOB OF KEEPING THE EGG WARM AND SAFE AFTER THE FEMALE LAYS IT. **The male balances the egg on his feet and covers it with soft feathered skin called a brood pouch.** During the 65 to 75 days before the eggs hatch, the male penguin eats nothing and will stand in the same place. **During that time, the male's only job is to protect and keep the egg warm.** For two months, the male guards the egg while the female penguin goes to the ocean in search of food. **The female eats as much as she can. After the egg hatches, the mother regurgitates the food for the baby to eat.** Then, it's the male penguin's turn to go eat!

Instant Genius

Emperor penguins are the world's largest living penguin species.

#63

What is the immune system's

primary job?

a. to build the body

b. to defend the body

c. to clean the body

Instant Genius

Your skin and hair are part of your immune system.

ANSWER: **b** **to defend the body**

THE IMMUNE SYSTEM DEFENDS THE BODY FROM INFECTION AND DISEASE. **It detects and attacks unhealthy cells and pathogens, such as viruses, bacteria, and fungi, which can make you sick.** It has two types of responses against harm: innate immunity and adaptive immunity. **The innate immune system acts quickly and can recognize and attack a pathogen that is present.** Say you cut your finger, and the wound gets inflamed. That's an example of the innate immune system at work as your body attempts to heal itself. **The adaptive immune system, on the other hand, is more specialized. It has the ability to recognize specific viruses and bacteria.** If an unknown pathogen enters the body, the adaptive immune system can learn to attack it, and even recognize it to zap again if it comes back.

135

A spinning disk from ancient Egypt with artwork depicting basenji dogs hunting gazelles

ANSWER: **True**

UNLIKE MOST DOGS, BASENJIS MAKE A SOUND THAT HAS BEEN BEST DESCRIBED AS "YODELING." They make a wide variety of howling sounds with different pitches. **But basenjis can't bark like other dog breeds. Why? They have a uniquely narrow larynx, which is an organ in the throat that contains the vocal cords.** The dogs originated in ancient Egypt and have been bred for thousands of years. Some researchers believe this was a trait encouraged through selective breeding (the process of choosing parents with specific characteristics to pass down to their offspring). **Egyptians may have wanted dogs that didn't bark so that they wouldn't attract predators such as lions to their villages and near livestock. No barking would also mean that basenjis didn't alert prey when helping hunters.**

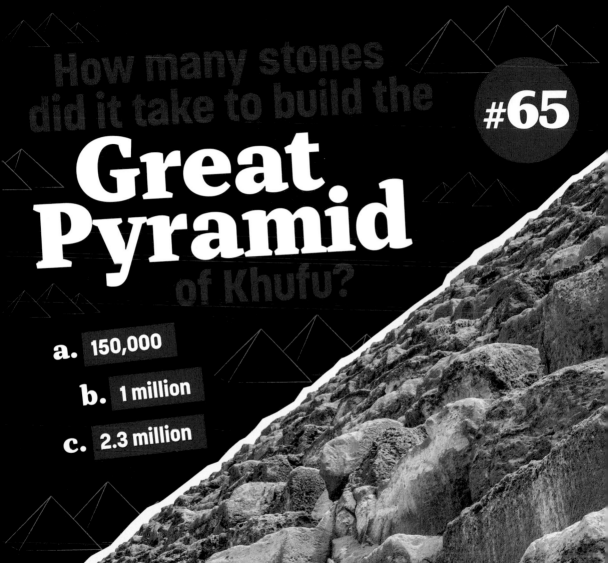

How many stones did it take to build the

Great Pyramid

of Khufu?

a. 150,000

b. 1 million

c. 2.3 million

ANSWER: C **2.3 million**

STANDING 481 FEET (147 M) TALL, THE GREAT PYRAMID OF KHUFU IN GIZA, EGYPT, IS ONE OF THE MOST IMPRESSIVE STRUCTURES IN THE WORLD. It was built around 4,500 years ago to house the tomb of an Egyptian pharaoh named Khufu. The ancient Egyptians believed that pharaohs became gods when they died, and the pyramids were built to show their devotion. **The Great Pyramid is made up of 2.3 million stones, some weighing as much as 15 tons (13.6 t), or twice as heavy as an elephant!** Historians today are baffled by how the ancient Egyptians were able to move thousands of tons of stone bricks hundreds of feet high without cranes or machinery. **What we do know is that the pyramid took decades to build and was probably made by many strong Egyptian workers.**

Instant Genius
Of the seven wonders of the ancient world, the Great Pyramid of Khufu is the only one still standing.

Which country has the
tallest men
on average?

a. **The Netherlands**

b. **Brazil**

c. **India**

#66

ANSWER: a

The Netherlands

ON AVERAGE, DUTCH MEN ARE TALLER THAN MEN OF ALL OTHER NATIONALITIES. **The average Dutch man is about 6 feet (1.8 m) tall, compared to 5 feet, 9 inches (1.75 m) in the United States.** The shortest men on average are found in East Timor, reaching heights of 5 feet, 3 inches (1.6 m) tall. People from different countries grow to different heights for several reasons. **One reason is genetics, or the DNA we inherit from our parents. Another reason is nutrition. Children who eat less protein or don't get all the proper nutrients while growing up tend to be shorter.** About 100 years ago, people around the world were shorter on average than they are today. In many countries, average heights have soared because of better nutrition.

Instant Genius

Shorter people generally live longer than taller people.

Which animal has the fastest heartbeat?

a. human

c. hummingbird

b. blue whale

ANSWER: **c** **hummingbird**

Instant Genius

The blue whale has the biggest heart of any animal, weighing about 400 pounds (181 kg).

OUR HEARTS BEAT ABOUT 60 TO 100 TIMES A MINUTE. That might seem like a lot, but consider this: **A hummingbird's heart beats 1,260 times a minute! A blue whale's heart, on the other hand, only beats between 2 and 37 times in the same amount of time. Our hearts are always beating, but they do not beat at a steady rate all the time.** Exercise makes our hearts beat faster because our bodies are doing more work and need more oxygen. **When we sleep, our bodies do less work, so our hearts beat slower.**

Baby carrots

are young carrots.

#68

143

ANSWER: False

DESPITE THEIR NAME, BABY CARROTS AREN'T YOUNG CARROTS, AND YOU CAN'T FIND THEM IN NATURE. **Carrots are grown underground and pulled out of the dirt once they're about 7 inches (18 cm) long.** Baby carrots are these same long carrots simply cut down into bite-size portions. **American carrot farmer Mike Yurosek invented them in the 1980s.** Before he came along, many carrots were considered too ugly for customers, so they went to waste. **To make the veggies more appealing, the smart farmer shaved them into cute, fun-size pieces that were a hit!** His simple invention led to huge increase in sales. Carrot farmers all over America began copying Yurosek, leading to the popular snack we still enjoy today.

Instant Genius

There once was a 17-foot (5-m)-tall carrot sculpture in San Diego, California, U.S.A.

True or False:

Sand tiger sharks

#69

attack each other in the womb.

Aliwal Shoal, Indian Ocean

Instant Genius

Sand tiger sharks are around 10 feet (3 m) long.

ANSWER: True

BEFORE A FEMALE SAND TIGER SHARK GIVES BIRTH, THERE ARE MULTIPLE OFFSPRING IN HER WOMB. **They fight in the womb to decide which is the strongest shark.** The strongest two fetuses will develop into full-size baby sharks, while the weaker ones stop competing for food and stop growing. **Because only the two strongest sharks are born, the population has a greater chance of surviving against predators and other threats.** The strong adults will go on to have their own baby sharks, which will be even stronger. **Though it may seem like extreme sibling rivalry, this process ensures that future generations will have the best chance of survival in the wild.**

#70

How much does it cost to create an astronaut's

space suit?

a. $1 million

b. $50 million

c. $250 million

$250 million

NASA HASN'T MADE ANY NEW SPACE SUITS SINCE 1974, BUT THE PRICE TO DO SO WOULD BE AROUND $250 MILLION PER SUIT! The space suits from 1974 cost around $15 to $22 million to make. Today, it would cost about $250 million. Why are they so expensive? **The suits are responsible for many jobs, such as protecting the astronauts from radiation, extreme temperatures, and particles floating around in space.** The suits also provide astronauts with oxygen, communication devices, and lights. **The most expensive part of the space suit is the backpack, or life-support system.** The backpack keeps the astronaut breathing by maintaining a constant temperature and pressure inside the suit, providing oxygen, and removing the exhaled carbon dioxide.

NOW YOU KNOW!

A space suit can withstand temperatures as hot as 250 °F (121 °C) and as cold as −250 °F (−156 °C).

Instant Genius

Space suits are white because the color reflects heat.

#71

True or False:

The largest big cat in the world is the jaguar.

149

ANSWER: False

THE LARGEST BIG CAT IN THE WORLD IS THE SIBERIAN TIGER.
The average male is 10.75 feet (3.3 m) long and weighs 660 pounds (300 kg)—about the same weight as three baby elephants. Females are smaller, at up to 9 feet (2.7 m) long and 370 pounds (168 kg). **These large tigers live mostly in eastern Russia, but a few are found in North Korea and China, too.** Elk, wild boars, and other larger mammals are the main prey for these fierce predators, and they need to eat about 60 pounds (27 kg) of meat a night to stay healthy. **To hunt, tigers lie down patiently in tall grasses, using their striped coats to camouflage themselves in their surroundings until they see their tasty prey.**

Instant Genius

The largest Siberian tiger ever documented was 845 pounds (383 kg).

What parts of the body generate **heat?**

#72

a. arteries and veins

b. hair and nails

c. organs and muscles

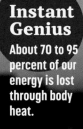

Instant Genius

About 70 to 95 percent of our energy is lost through body heat.

ANSWER: C **organs and muscles**

TO MAINTAIN A CONSTANT AND HEALTHY BODY TEMPERATURE, MAMMALS DEPEND ON A SYSTEM CALLED THERMOREGULATION, WHICH HELPS OUR MUSCLES AND ORGANS GENERATE BODY HEAT. **Even when the temperature of our outside environment changes, we are able to maintain a constant body temperature.** If the outside temperature gets too cold or too hot, our brain will send signals to our muscles and organs to either shiver if we are too cold or sweat if we are too hot. **Humans usually keep their internal temperature between 97 °F and 99 °F (36 °C–37 °C).** Any temperature higher or lower than this could signify infection or some other illness, such as the flu or hypothermia, and can be damaging to our organs. **The more our muscles work, the more body heat we give off.**

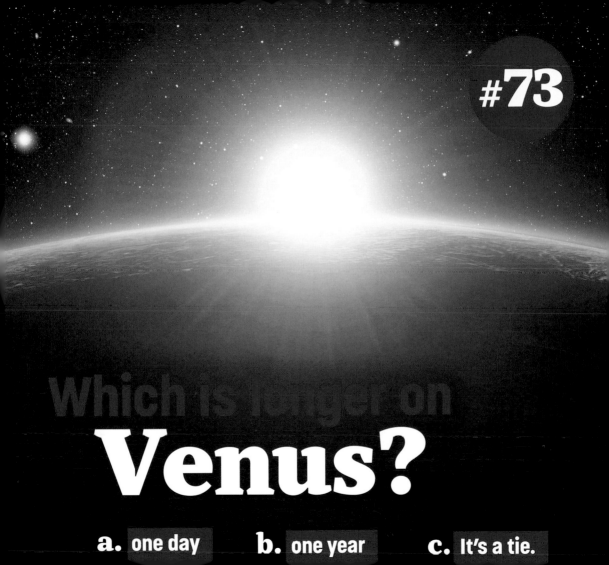

#73

Which is longer on

Venus?

a. one day   b. one year   c. It's a tie.

ANSWER: **a** **one day**

A PLANET COMPLETES A DAY WHEN IT MAKES A FULL 360-DEGREE ROTATION AROUND ITS AXIS. A planet completes a year when it makes one full revolution around the sun. Venus rotates very slowly on its axis compared with Earth. **It takes Venus 243 Earth days to complete one day of its own. That's a 5,832-hour day!** Just one night on Venus is 108 days on Earth. Venus also revolves around the sun faster than it spins on its own axis, so one year on Venus is about 225 days on Earth, meaning a year on Venus is 18 days shorter than a day on Venus!

Instant Genius

Venus's atmosphere contains no oxygen.

#74

The **brain**

uses 20 percent of the body's oxygen and blood supply.

NOW
YOU KNOW!
Your brain can generate
about 23 watts of power.
That's enough energy to
power a lightbulb!

ANSWER: True

THE BRAIN MAKES UP ONLY 2 PERCENT OF OUR BODY MASS, YET IT USES UP TO 20 PERCENT OF THE BODY'S BLOOD AND OXYGEN SUPPLY. Brains need this huge supply to power the rest of the body. **Our brains are made up of neurons, which send signals back to various parts of the brain and the entire body.** These signals are how we move our muscles, store memories, think, and feel emotions. **To do all these jobs, neurons need a constant supply of oxygen. Arteries and capillaries are the blood vessels that lead oxygen to the brain**. If your brain is low on oxygen, blood flow to the brain will increase, carrying oxygen in blood cells so the brain can get the oxygen it needs.

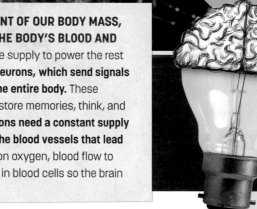

How far can a
honeybee
fly in one day?

a. 2 miles (3 km)   **b.** 5 miles (8 km)

c. 7 miles (11 km)

Bees pollinate a third of the food that we eat.

ANSWER: **b** 5 miles (8 km)

NOW YOU KNOW!
The queen honeybee is the largest bee in the colony. She also has a lot to do: During her busiest time, the queen honeybee lays up to 2,000 eggs a day.

WHEN FORAGING, A SINGLE HONEYBEE CAN FLY UP TO 5 MILES (8 KM) IN A DAY. However, it is very unlikely that a bee would have to fly that far because food is usually within 1 mile (1.6 km) of the bee's hive. When setting out in search of food, bees fly at a speed of 15 to 20 miles an hour (24–32 kmh). **Weighed down with nectar and pollen they've collected from flowers and plants for the hive, their travel slows to about 12 miles an hour (19 kmh).** On average, a honeybee visits between 50 and 100 flowers per trip out of the hive. That's something to buzz about!

True or False:

#76

All animals get
goose bumps.

Can I borrow your sweatshirt?

159

ANSWER: **False**

NOW YOU KNOW!
Goose bumps are also called "gooseflesh" because the skin resembles a plucked bird.

ONLY MAMMALS GET GOOSE BUMPS. When a mammal's body gets cold, the muscles around the hair follicles contract. This causes the body hair to stand up straight and create a blanket around the skin to produce warmth. **Because humans have less hair than, let's say, chimps or dogs, it's easier to see this reaction because the skin is exposed.** Cold is not the only cause though. Fear and, according to a survey, even listening to music can cause goose bumps.

How does a
snail
make its own shell?

a. It produces proteins and minerals.

b. It hardens its skin.

c. It doesn't—it moves into a shell it finds.

ANSWER: a

It produces proteins and minerals.

SNAILS ARE PART OF A GROUP OF ORGANISMS CALLED MOLLUSKS. Snails and other shelled mollusks make their own shells by biomineralization, the process through which an organism makes minerals. These minerals form the snail's shell, which begins to grow before a baby snail is even born. **Mollusk shells are made of about 95 to 99 percent minerals (mostly calcium carbonate), with the remaining percentage made of proteins.** Snails get most of the minerals they need to make their shells from the water they drink. The minerals are held together with proteins, making the shells strong yet lightweight. **As snails grow, their shells grow with them, including the layers of the spiral.**

Instant Genius
If you put a shell in vinegar, it will dissolve.

#78

True or False:

Lightning

is caused
by storms in space

Supercell thunderstorm, Kansas

Instant Genius
Lightning can be five times hotter than the surface of the sun.

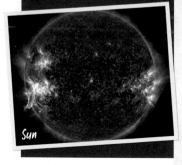
Sun

ANSWER: **False**

LIGHTNING HAPPENS WHEN WATER DROPLETS RUB TOGETHER IN A STORM CLOUD AND CREATE A STATIC CHARGE, WHICH CAUSES THE TOP HALF OF THE CLOUD TO BE POSITIVELY CHARGED AND THE BOTTOM HALF TO BE NEGATIVELY CHARGED. As these opposite forces become stronger, they repel each other more strongly, like two magnets pushing apart. Eventually the negative charge tries to reach the ground, which is positively charged during a storm. **When the charges become too powerful, the cloud releases the negative charge in the form of lightning.** The air around the lightning strike suddenly heats to very high temperatures, and the initial shock wave creates a cracking sound. **What follows is the rumbling sound we know as thunder, which is the air vibrating after the shock of the strike.**

Skeletal muscles
always come in pairs.

#79

ANSWER: True

SKELETAL MUSCLES ARE ONE OF THREE TYPES OF MUSCLES IN OUR BODY. They're grouped together in pairs and attached to our bones by our tendons, so when one muscle in a pair contracts, the other relaxes. Skeletal muscles can only pull in one direction, so they must work in pairs to move back and forth. For example, when you bend your arm and bring the lower part to your bicep in the upper part, your bicep is doing the work of pulling up your lower arm. Then the tricep muscle in your upper arm takes over to do the work of lowering the arm. If skeletal muscles did not occur in pairs, it wouldn't be possible to both bend and straighten.

Instant Genius

The human body contains more than 600 muscles.

NOW YOU KNOW!

The word *muscle* comes from the Latin word meaning "little mouse."

True or False:

Lemurs and **humans** are in the same family.

#80

Did we meet at the family reunion?

ANSWER: **True**

HUMANS AND LEMURS ARE BOTH IN THE FAMILY OF PRIMATES. Primates have three major things in common. They all have two eyes that act like binoculars to see distance, hands and feet that can grasp things such as food or tools, and large areas in the brain that give them the ability to reason and think creatively. However, lemurs and humans are different types of primates. Humans are anthropoids, which are more developed primates. **Lemurs are prosimians, which means they rely more on their sense of smell than sight and cannot use their fingers in the specialized way that humans can.**

Instant Genius

Sifakas, a type of lemur, can jump more than 30 feet (9 m) in a single bound.

Which is the most populated

continent?

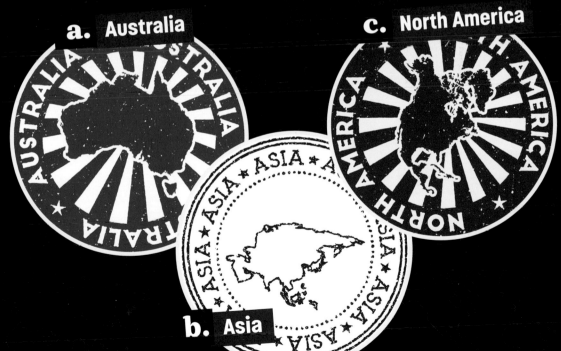

a. Australia

b. Asia

c. North America

Ho Chi Minh City, Vietnam

ANSWER: b Asia

ASIA IS THE MOST POPULATED CONTINENT IN THE WORLD—BY FAR.
More people live in Asia than in all other continents combined! **Asia has a population of more than 4.7 billion people.** The second most populated continent is Africa, which has around 1.4 billion people. **Asia is also the largest continent in the world, making up about 30 percent of Earth's land area.** Many countries in Asia have a very high population density, which means a lot of people live very close together. **Singapore, with more than 21,000 people per square mile (8,358 per sq km), has the highest population density on the continent.**

Instant Genius

With two people per square mile, Mongolia has the lowest population density of any independent country.

#82

The
sun
is yellow.

171

ANSWER: **False**

THE SUN IS A MASSIVE BALL OF GASES. When all these gases collide, the reaction creates something called nuclear fusion. **This makes the sun very hot and produces enormous amounts of light. The color of this light is white because it is a combination of all colors in the spectrum.** So why does the sun appear yellow to us? **Each color has a different wavelength. The color blue, for example, has a very short wavelength, whereas red, yellow, and orange have longer wavelengths.** A shorter wavelength means higher energy and faster-moving particles. Because blue light has faster-moving particles, it scatters before it reaches us, so it is no longer visible. **The wavelength that reaches us is yellow.**

Bald eagles

are, indeed, bald.

#83

THE REASON THESE BIRDS ARE CALLED "BALD EAGLES" IS NOT BECAUSE THEY ARE MISSING FEATHERS ON THEIR HEADS. The name comes from the old English word *balde*, which means "white." Bald eagles are magnificent birds of prey that use their large 2-inch (5-cm)-long talons to catch fish and steal prey from other predators. **A pair of bald eagles mate for life. They build a large nest for their eggs, and return to the same one every year, adding new material each time to make it bigger.** A nest can get so huge that its weight can cause the tree it's in to topple over.

NOW YOU KNOW!
The wingspan of a bald eagle is 6 to 7 feet (1.8–2.1 m) across. This long wingspan allows the birds to fly at speeds of 30 miles an hour (48 kmh).

What percentage of Saudia Arabia is desert?

a. 50 percent **b.** 75 percent

c. 95 percent

#84

Instant Genius

Winds in the Arabian Desert can reach up to 30 miles an hour (48 kmh).

ANSWER: C **95 percent**

Flint tools such as hand axes from more than 100,000 years ago have been found in the Arabian Desert.

THERE ARE TWO DESERTS IN SAUDI ARABIA: THE RUB' AL-KHALI IN THE SOUTH AND THE AL-NAFŪD IN THE NORTH. Together, they make up the greater Arabian Desert, which covers 95 percent of Saudi Arabia. The Arabian Desert is the second largest subtropical desert on Earth, covering nearly 900,000 square miles (2.3 million sq km) of land and running through nine countries. **The Al-Nafūd desert is famous for its massive sand dunes, some reaching more than 100 feet (30 m) tall. The Rub' al-Khali is the biggest desert on the Arabian Peninsula and one of the driest regions in the world.** On average, the desert receives less than 1 inch (25 mm) of rain per year, and temperatures here can reach 124 °F (51 °C). This desert also has the largest expanse of continuous sand dunes.

It's impossible to fold a **piece of paper** in half more than seven times.

ANSWER: False

IF YOU TOOK A PIECE OF NOTEBOOK PAPER AND STARTED FOLDING, YOU PROBABLY WOULDN'T BE ABLE TO GET PAST FIVE OR SIX FOLDS. In fact, it is unlikely that anyone could fold a piece of notebook paper in half more than seven times because the thickness of paper increases as you fold it. **But there is a trick: Start with a long and thin piece of paper, which will give you more folds because of its shape.** The paper must be four times longer than it is wide. High school student Britney Gallivan set the record for the most times a piece of paper has been folded in half. Gallivan managed 12 folds using a piece of toilet paper 4,000 feet (1,219 m) long!

#86

True or False:

Speech recognition technology is helping researchers understand volcanoes.

179

Mount Etna, Italy

ANSWER: **True**

IN THE PAST, SCIENTISTS HAVE TRIED TO UNDERSTAND VOLCANIC BEHAVIOR BY LOOKING AT A VOLCANO'S GEOGRAPHIC LOCATION AND HISTORY, AND THE BEHAVIOR OF THE MAGMA UNDERNEATH. But none of these methods are certain and volcanic eruptions can often be unexpected. Scientists are using speech recognition technology—which uses computers to translate human speech into written text— to better predict volcanic activity. **The technology can detect and record patterns of seismic activity, which is the sudden release of energy from the breaking of Earth's crust or upper mantle, in the same way it can pick up and record patterns in speech.** Scientists can then analyze the recorded data to estimate the timing of the next volcanic eruption.

#87

True or False:

Elephant tusks

are actually teeth.

Is there spinach stuck on my tusk!

181

ANSWER: True

TUSKS ARE ACTUALLY VERY LONG TEETH. The ivory tusk is made of dentin and covered in enamel, much like a human tooth. Elephants use their tusks to dig, lift objects, defend themselves against predators, and eat. **All African elephants have tusks, but only male Asian elephants have tusks.** Elephant tusks are very beautiful, which has made these large animals vulnerable. **Every year, poachers—people who illegally hunt animals—kill thousands of elephants to make and sell jewelry and trinkets from their tusks.** Thank goodness countries in Africa and Asia have taken notice of the harmful practices, leading to positive change. **Rangers in Africa now patrol areas to protect elephants, and China banned the ivory trade and made selling ivory illegal.**

Instant Genius
Adult elephants have no natural predators.

True or False:

#88

The
Mona Lisa
lost her
eyebrows.

French engineer and founder of Lumiere Technology, Pascal Cotte

ANSWER: **True**

IN THE EARLY 1500s, LEONARDO DA VINCI PAINTED AN ITALIAN WOMAN NAMED LISA GHERARDINI, AND THE *MONA LISA* WAS BORN. But as paintings age, they tend to chip and fade. Because the *Mona Lisa* is about 500 years old, it likely looks a little different today. Knowing this, a French engineer wanted to know what the woman may have looked like when she was newly painted. **He developed a camera to take extremely detailed scans of the painting. With these scans, he could see brushstrokes of paint that was no longer there.** Today, if you look at the woman in the painting, you'll notice she doesn't have any eyebrows or lashes. **What the engineer discovered, however, is that the *Mona Lisa* used to have both!**

Instant Genius
The *Mona Lisa*, stolen in 1911, was missing for two years.

Which two countries share the longest land border?

a. Argentina and Chile

c. United States and Canada

b. Russia and China

185

Instant Genius

The U.S. state with the longest coastline is Alaska.

UNITED STATES CANADA

INTERNATIONAL BOUNDARY LINE

NOW YOU KNOW!

Canada is the second largest country in the world after Russia, yet it only has 0.5 percent of the world's population. Why?

ANSWER: **c**

United States and Canada

THOUGH NEITHER CANADA NOR THE UNITED STATES IS THE LONGEST COUNTRY IN THE WORLD (THAT RECORD BELONGS TO CHILE), THEY SHARE THE LONGEST LAND BORDER OF ANY TWO COUNTRIES. Their border includes two parts: the stretch of land between Canada and the Lower 48 states, plus the border between the state of Alaska and northwest Canada. Altogether, the border is 5,524 miles (8,890 km) long. In comparison, the border between Russia and China is 2,568 miles (4,133 km) long, and the border between Argentina and Chile is 3,298 miles (5,308 km) long.

Emerald Lake, Yukon, Canada

#90

True or False:

It's impossible to **breathe** and **swallow** at the same time.

ANSWER: True

BREATHING AND SWALLOWING AT THE SAME TIME IS IMPOSSIBLE. That's because the throat has two parts with two different functions that take turns. This coordination prevents air from going into the stomach, and liquid and food from going into the lungs. When we're breathing, clean air flows down the trachea, at the front of the throat, then enters the lungs. As for swallowing, food and water go down the esophagus, located at the back of the throat, before food is moved into the stomach to be digested. **A muscle called the epiglottis moves back and forth to cover one "pipe" so that the other can function.** Sometimes it accidentally lets food or liquid particles into the trachea. **That's why, when you cough after eating or drinking, someone might say, "It went down the wrong pipe."**

Bats
are shy.

Hello?

Battambang Bat Cave, Cambodia

ANSWER: **False**

Some bat species live in colonies with more than 50 million members!

THERE ARE 18 DIFFERENT BAT FAMILIES AND MORE THAN 900 SPECIES. Bats are nocturnal and feed at night, which might make them seem rare to humans. But bats are very common and are found across the world, except in Antarctica and the Arctic. **They are also very social creatures within their groups, communicating with a language of different vocalizations.** In fact, one researcher has identified more than 50 distinct call types, from sharp whispers to loud hollers. **Most bat species travel and hunt together.** Some have even been seen splitting into social hierarchies—a ranking of groups by their importance—in their roosts.

Teeth are considered part of which body system?

#92

b. skeletal system

a. digestive system

c. nervous system

skeletal system

TEETH ARE CONSIDERED PART OF THE SKELETAL SYSTEM, EVEN THOUGH THEY ARE NOT ACTUALLY BONE. Our teeth are made of enamel, dentin, and pulp. **Enamel is the outermost part of the tooth and the strongest substance in our bodies, which comes in handy for chewing food every day.** It is a thin protective layer that surrounds the exposed part of our tooth, which is called the crown. Enamel allows the tooth to withstand hard, crunchy food. **Dentin, the layer directly under the enamel, makes up most of the tooth.** Like enamel, dentin is also hard. The pulp is the innermost layer of the tooth and is the softest part. **Pulp is made of tissue, nerves, and blood vessels.**

Instant Genius

Adults usually have 12 more teeth than children.

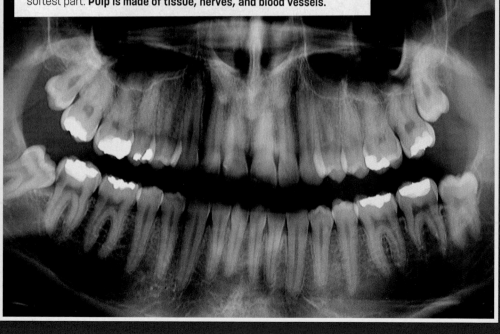

ANSWER: **a** | **a chimpanzee**

THE AVERAGE HUMAN MALE IS 5 FEET, 9 INCHES (1.75 M) TALL AND WEIGHS ABOUT 200 POUNDS (91 KG) WHEREAS THE AVERAGE MALE CHIMPANZEE IS 3 FEET (1 M) TALL AND WEIGHS 120 POUNDS (54 KG). Given these facts, it might seem like the human would be stronger. **Though human males may have bigger bodies, male chimpanzees are 1.5 times stronger than humans when it comes to jumping and pulling.** The reason for this is the way a chimp's muscles are built. In both chimps and humans, strength comes from the muscle fibers closest to the bone. Chimps have more of this type of muscle. **By having denser muscle near the bone, chimps can use more force in short bursts.** For example, a chimp using a hammer would strike harder than a man because of the extra muscle power.

True or False:

All **insects** have six legs.

#94

ANSWER: True

THINK ABOUT ANTS, BEETLES, AND BEES. What do they all have in common? **All insects have exactly six legs. They also have two antennae, an abdomen, and a thorax, which is the body part between the head and the abdomen.** If a bug is missing any one of these body parts, or has more than six legs, it's probably a spider or some other kind of creepy-crawly. Like other kinds of bugs, insects have many different jobs. **Some pollinate plants, while others produce materials such as honey, wax, and silk. Some even eat other bugs, keeping the ecosystem in check.**

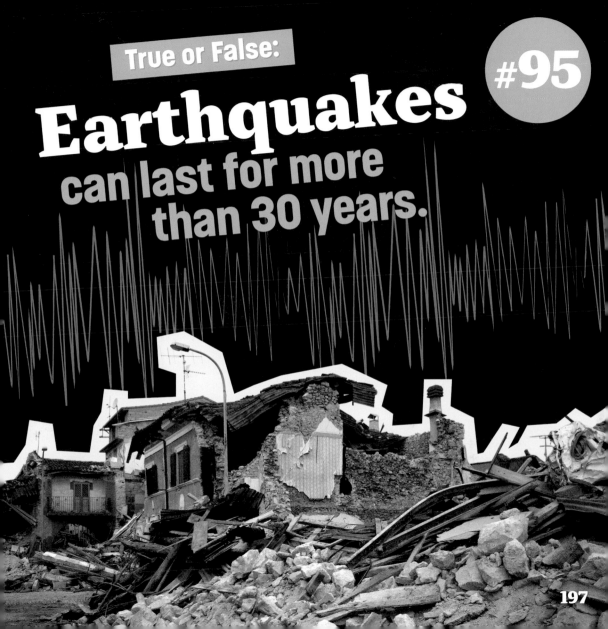

True or False:

Earthquakes

can last for more than 30 years.

ANSWER: **True**

A large crack in the ground caused by an earthquake

BEGINNING IN 1829, AN EARTHQUAKE IN INDONESIA LASTED FOR 32 YEARS, MAKING IT THE LONGEST-LASTING EARTHQUAKE ON RECORD. Earthquakes happen because our planet is divided into several tectonic plates, which are large, interlocking chunks of rock that make up Earth's crust. Underneath the crust, magma is constantly shifting. **This makes the plates move constantly, but very slowly.** As the plates push against each other, tension builds up. **An earthquake is the sudden release of tension in Earth's crust, which causes the ground to shake.** The 32-year quake was something called a slow quake, which is an earthquake in slow motion. Slow quakes are so slow and unnoticeable that scientists didn't know they existed until the late 1990s!

Instant Genius

Scientists have measured moonquakes on the moon.

True or False:

Alaska, U.S.A., has fewer **caribou** than people.

#96

Anyone seen Santa Claus?

199

Instant Genius

Anchorage, the biggest city in Alaska, has about 290,000 people.

ANSWER: **False**

ALASKA HAS ABOUT 700,000 PEOPLE AND NEARLY 1 MILLION CARIBOU. You may be familiar with the caribou's other name—reindeer, which is what it's called in Europe. **In Alaska and Canada, reindeer are domesticated caribou that are used to living around people. The wild ones are simply called caribou.** Caribou are related to deer, but unlike deer, both male and female caribou grow antlers and have paddle-like feet to help them swim in water and walk in snow. Babies weigh about 13 pounds (6 kg) at birth and weigh up to 400 pounds (181 kg) when fully grown. **There are several different subspecies of caribou. In Alaska, the barren-ground caribou is the main subspecies, named after the type of terrain the caribou live on.** There is also a small number of woodland caribou.

NOW YOU KNOW!

Alaska has more men than women—but the rest of the United States has more women than men.

Why don't electric planes exist?

a. The batteries would be too heavy.

b. They're more likely to get struck by lightning.

c. The airline industry won't allow it.

Instant Genius

About 5,000 airplanes are flying over the United States at any moment.

ANSWER: a **The batteries would be too heavy.**

PEOPLE HAVE BEEN FLYING ON AIRPLANES FOR MORE THAN A HUNDRED YEARS. They are a fast, efficient, and safe way to travel. However, air travel takes a toll on the environment. Scientists are trying to figure out a greener solution. **Electric-powered planes aren't currently an option because the batteries would be too heavy for flight. An airplane battery would be about 30 times heavier than a can of jet fuel that provides the same amount of energy.** However, a hybrid plane may be an alternative, and researchers are working on it! Like hybrid cars, hybrid planes would combine the use of electric batteries and fuel. **This would reduce the environmental impact of airplanes and keep them light enough to fly.**

#98

How many muscles does it take to

walk one step?

a. **20**

b. **200**

c. **2,000**

One foot in front of the other...

TO WALK EVEN ONE STEP, 200 DIFFERENT MUSCLES TEAM UP TO GET THE JOB DONE. The first groups of muscles are the quadriceps, which are located in the front of the upper thighs, and the hamstrings, which are located at the back of the thighs. These are the biggest muscles in the legs, and they move the legs forward and backward. The calf muscles propel the legs forward. **Then a set of muscles located near your shins are used to help raise the foot so that it doesn't scrape on the ground mid-step.** Muscles keep the body upright by pulling against gravity. **By contracting to shorten or lengthen, muscles are responsible for every single movement the body makes.**

quadriceps

hamstrings

calf

Instant Genius

A typical pair of sneakers lasts for 500 miles (805 km) of walking.

204

Insects
live in the ocean.

Pond skater

OVER TIME, INSECTS HAVE COME TO LIVE IN MANY ECOSYSTEMS ACROSS THE GLOBE, INCLUDING HOSTILE ENVIRONMENTS LIKE BLISTERING DESERTS AND THE FROZEN TUNDRA. The only exception to this is the ocean. **The main reason that there are no insects in the ocean is because insects do not have lungs.** Insects breathe through tubes and openings in their bodies called spiracles. **Unlike fish, which all have gills, insects cannot filter the air from the water.** Although some insects can glide across the water or even survive underwater, they can only do so for a short time.

Instant Genius
All insects are cold-blooded.

A tiger beetle at the water's surface

What is the largest **solid organ** organ inside your body?

a. liver

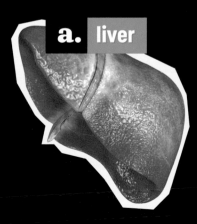

b. brain

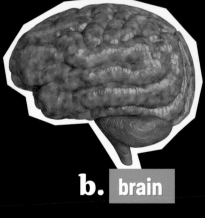

c. heart

Scanning electron microscopy (SEM) of a fractured bile duct

ANSWER: a liver

THE LIVER WEIGHS 3 TO 3.5 POUNDS (1.4–1.6 KG), ROUGHLY THE SIZE OF A FOOTBALL. It holds about 13 percent of the body's blood supply at any given moment. All of the blood leaving the stomach and intestines travels here. **By the time it reaches the liver, it's rich with nutrients and toxins from the food we eat.** The liver breaks down the toxins and regulates our blood sugar levels. If our sugar levels are too high, the liver will remove sugar from our bloodstream and convert it into glycogen, which is like backup fuel that can be saved for later. **The liver also creates a protein that helps prevent blood from clotting. With so many tasks to keep our blood healthy, it is no surprise that it's the biggest solid organ.**

Instant Genius
The liver has more than 500 identified functions.

#101

How much of the
**solar
system's
mass**
does the sun take up?

a. 50.27 percent

b. 75.54 percent

c. 99.86 percent

ANSWER: C **99.86 percent**

THOUGH NOT THE BIGGEST STAR IN OUR GALAXY, THE SUN IS THE LARGEST OBJECT IN OUR SOLAR SYSTEM. **About 1.3 million Earths can fit inside it.** The sun's mass is about 330,000 times greater than Earth's. **It is so large that it takes 170,000 years for energy from its core to reach its own surface.** As the sun gets older, it also slowly expands. Eventually it will expand far enough to swallow Mercury, Venus, and maybe even Earth—but that will not happen for billions of years.

Spot the 7 Random Differences:

Turn to page 215 for the answers!

Index

Photo Credits

Credits

Visit us on the Web! **rhcbooks.com**

Educators and librarians, for a variety of teaching tools, visit us
at **RHTeachersLibrarians.com**

Library of Congress Cataloging-in-Publication Data is available
upon request.
ISBN 978-0-593-51634-8 (trade)
ISBN 978-0-593-51635-5 (lib. bdg.)
ISBN 978-0-593-51636-2 (ebook)

COVER PHOTO CREDITS:
Front Cover Photo: Shutterstock.
Back Cover Photo: Dreamstime.

MANUFACTURED IN ITALY
10 9 8 7 6 5 4 3 2 1
First Edition

Produced by Fun Factory Press, LLC, in association with
Potomac Global Media, LLC.

The publisher would like to thank the following people for their
contributions to this book: Melina Gerosa Bellows, President,
Fun Factory Press, and Series Creator and Author; Priyanka
Lamichhane, Editor and Project Manager; Chad Tomlinson, Art
Director; Jane Sunderland, Copy Editor; Mary Stephanos, Fact-
checker; Potomac Global Media: Kevin Mulroy, Publisher; Barbara
Brownell Grogan, Editor in Chief; Christopher L. Mazzatenta,
Designer; Susannah Jayes and Ellen Dupont, Picture Researchers;
Jane Sunderland and Heather McElwain, Contributing Editors.

BRIGHT
MATTER
BOOKS

TOTALLY
RANDOM
KIDS